Headley's Past in

Headley's

Past in

Pictures

Compiled by
John Owen Smith

Headley's Past in Pictures
First published December 1999
Reprinted with minor additions and amendments February 2000
Republished with further minor additions and amendments 2003

Typeset and published by John Owen Smith
19 Kay Crescent, Headley Down, Hampshire GU35 8AH

Tel: 01428 712892 – Fax: 08700 516554
wordsmith@johnowensmith.co.uk
www.johnowensmith.co.uk/

ISBN 1-873855-27-3

Printed and bound by Antony Rowe Ltd, Eastbourne

Publisher's Note

This is the first in a series of publications through which we intend to illustrate the history of the parish of Headley from different perspectives. In this book, we show some of the buildings, locations and features which have defined the character of the parish up to the middle of the twentieth century. Other books in the series look in more detail at its people and societies, and at more recent changes to its architecture and landscape.

In this book you are taken on a tour of the parish by means of three journeys —the first around the centre of Headley and Arford, the second to Headley Down and beyond, and the third along the River Wey and its tributaries. In doing so, we venture occasionally outside today's civil parish boundaries—but that too is all part of the history of Headley.

Further information on the history of Headley may be found on the Internet at website <www.headley-village.com/history/>

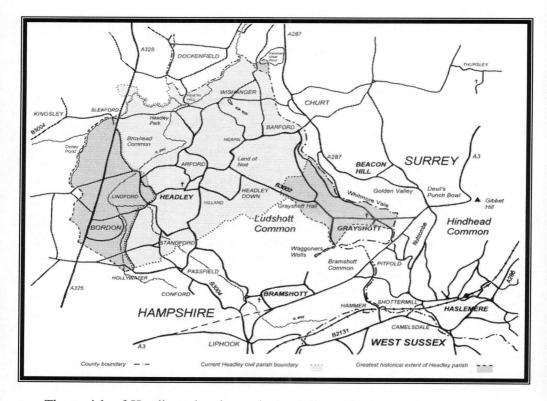

The parish of Headley, showing today's civil parish (light shading), and the greatest extent of the parish as it was up until the start of the 20th century (darker shading).

In 1902, Grayshott became an independent parish; in 1929, the parish of Whitehill was formed taking away Bordon and Lindford; and in 1991, the south bank of Frensham Great Pond became part of Surrey.

Contents

ର ର ର

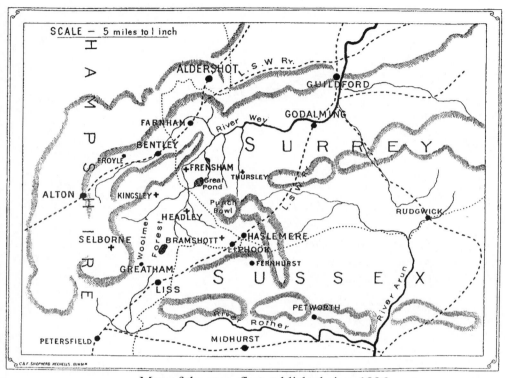

SCALE — 5 miles to 1 inch

Map of the area, first published circa 1896
in *A Souvenir of Headley* written by Charles H. Beck
(slightly reduced in scale)

*There are a number of inaccuracies shown on this map, for example
the county boundary at the time should have gone through Frensham
Great Pond, and Liphook is placed too near to Haslemere.*

Introduction

Since this is a history book, it seems fitting to use as an introduction some relevant passages from *A Souvenir of Headley*, published around 1896 by Charles H. Beck, then head teacher at the Holme School:—

Nestling amid the hills which form the western extremity of the South Downs, and half hidden by semi-forests of birch, beech and giant pine, lies the village of Headley—just where the counties of Hampshire, Sussex and Surrey meet. The prospect is essentially one of hill and dale—cheerful in winter, for evergreens abound, and surprisingly delightful in summer, when the vividly bright blossoms of the gorse and broom are mellowed by the miles of purple heather—seen nowhere to greater perfection. It is said that Hampshire will be the last county in England to retain its natural wild beauty, and judging from much of its soil this seems likely. Where houses have sprung up, they are mostly detached, and though many of them do not claim any notice for their architectural merits, they are charmingly situated. The artist will find some delightful studies in the thatched cottages, and the further he goes from beaten tracks the better will he be repaid.

Still, over a hundred years later, we can recognise this as a description of our parish, though the thatch has mostly disappeared. The author continues …

Headley enjoys a delightfully fresh and dry atmosphere, being situated on a gravelly soil some 326 to 600 feet above the sea-level. The water is of great purity, though somewhat hard. The rainfall is about 30 inches, as compared with 24 for London, 35 to 40 for Southampton, and 40 to 50 in the West of England. The winters are generally comparatively mild, yet while the snow rarely lies on the ground for any considerable time, the frosts are keen.

Mr Beck then goes on to describe the extent of the parish and its employment in 1896:—

The Parish of Headley covers an area of nearly 11 square miles, and besides the village of Headley proper, contains the hamlets of Lindford, Standford, and Grayshott. The population is about 1,800 mainly supported by farming. Hops are an important crop, and a visit to the hop-fields during the harvesting will be found very interesting. This plant seems to delight in the nature of the soil, and well repays the care bestowed upon it. Geese rearing was the chief employment years ago, and still on the lower commons large numbers are bred. An inferior kind of peat, together with bavins (the local name for faggots), forms the fuel for the poorer class. To the eyes of a northerner the huge stacks of firewood appear ridiculous, though he wonders more at the rapid rate these stacks disappear, and relishes the flavour they give to the celebrated "Hampshire bacon."

These were the days before Bordon Camp was built, and before Grayshott split away to become its own parish. The area of the civil parish has now reduced to only 7.6 square miles, and the population has risen to over 5,500. Hops are no longer grown, nor is geese rearing a major source of employment—though they are still to be found threading their way through traffic near Headley Mill pond. As to the conditions in 1896, we see that ...

Headley has no market, but there are markets held at Farnham (Thursday), Guildford (Tuesday) and Petersfield (every alternate Wednesday). Liphook is the nearest station (L. & S. W. R. Portsmouth, direct route), four and a half miles distant, Bentley being about six miles. Several carriers run between these places and are a great convenience, although the Stores in the village are good. The Postal and Telegraph Office is in the centre of the parish. There are eight inns, yet no hotel. The want of better accommodation for visitors prevents this charming place being more widely known, though private apartments may be obtained. Doubtless the large landowners are not anxious to see visitors, but it is a certain fact that there is a good opening for a hotel managed economically. Now that inland resorts are more sought, it is likely the dry situation, pure water, and wild scenery of Headley will more than ever prove attractive to those who love nature at her best.

He then recommends a number of walks and carriage rides from Headley—but remember, this is 1896.

A walk, or gentle drive, over the river at Standford to Blackmoor, visiting the church and estate of Earl Selborne, working round Woolmer Pond (so highly spoken of by Gilbert White, and interesting if only for the Roman coins found there), and returning through Conford, will prove a delightful outing. This neighbourhood is enlivened in August by the military camps on the large tracks of common land held by the War Department. The military high-road from Aldershot to Portsmouth skirts this district.

Another pleasant drive, to Frensham Pond, must certainly be undertaken. Taking the road by Wishanger Lodge, a spot exceedingly pretty, the Pond is soon reached. It covers an area of 103 acres, and is well stocked with pike, perch, tench, carp, and eels. A good fleet of boats is available, and a hotel rests at the edge of the lake. The road at Simmondstone should then be taken, when Hampshire lanes will be seen at their best, and a pleasant ride through Hearn will lead to Headley.

There are many gentle walks closer at hand which will soon be discovered, but one to Headley Park must be mentioned. Passing through that part of the village known as Arford, the road lies at the side of a little valley, the Hanger. This name is common in Hampshire, and is applied to those roads on the sides of valleys overhung with trees. Here primroses abound, the delicious "meadowsweet" fills the air with fragrance and the thrush and nightingale are heard to perfection.

The common snake (coluber natrix) is found here, and in most of the woods around—the author caught a fine specimen two years ago, about 36 inches long. In some of the less frequented parts the adder is still to be found. The road leads to the left, then by Headley Wood estate, across the fields to Headley Park. Giant firs and exceptionally tall bracken are special features. Rabbits are plentiful, and the magpie is by no means scarce. The home of Sir R. S. Wright stands a little to the north, and commands a lovely view.

Turning to the left, skirting the woods, the path leads across the wildest of commons to Lindford, and thence to Headley village.

In whichever way a journey is taken, the high banks at the roadside are very striking. The roots of the trees are often laid bare, forming fantastic shapes among the rocky strata, the polypodium vulgaris, ever fresh and green, converting these bits of loveliness into fairy gardens. It is also noticed that the free-stone so plentifully scattered in this district is largely used in building, being somewhat soft when first quarried, but hardening on exposure to the atmosphere. The curious nail-like ornamentation of some of the older buildings is produced by fragments of bluish-grey iron-stone being stuck in the mortar. A good example of this quaint custom is to be seen in the Headley school-house.

More need not be said of a district so full of beauty, so richly diversified, for the lover of rural peace and pleasure will have learnt enough to wish for more. At least that such may be the case is the earnest desire of the Author.

To which this modern author can only echo 'Amen.'

Part 1

High Street to Arford

HIGH STREET TO ARFORD

The High Street in Headley lies on high ground between the valleys of the River Wey and the Arford stream, and was simply called The Street in past times. The focal point of the parish, here we have the parish church of All Saints, its rectory and tithe barn, the *Holly Bush* inn, and the commemorative chestnut tree planted at the triangular road junction.

Over the years, there have been several shops and tradesmen operating here, but, as with so many rural communities, these have now dwindled to a mere handful.

In this first section of the book, we make a circular tour from the High Street, down Long Cross Hill to Arford, and back again by way of the Village Green, side-stepping to include a couple of properties, *Benifold* and *The Grange*, each of which has its own interesting story to tell.

Arford is the second centre of Headley, and was the location of further shops and tradesmen—sadly all now disappeared except for the *Crown*. However, with its stone walls and winding roads, it remains perhaps one of the most picturesque parts of the parish.

You will find further historical information on parts of this tour in 'To the Ar and Back,' written in 1992 by Joyce Stevens.

All Saints' Church in 1875

All Saints' Church had been almost completely rebuilt using largely existing materials in 1859, sixteen years before this picture was taken. This followed a fire in May 1836 which had destroyed the previous wooden-shingled spire (see sketch on right) and damaged part of the building.

This drawing of the Church, as it was according to the best of Henry Knight's recollection, is to be found in Macmillan's edition of White's Selborne (1875), illustrated by Mrs Laverty's father, Professor De la Motte.

The Church, Headley.

CREEPING IVY—

From a few strands visible on the photograph of 1875 (see previous page), the church eventually became almost completely covered in ivy. Pictures on this page show steady encroachment up the tower over the years. The ivy growth was finally removed by 1931, and is now kept well under control.

All Saints Church in 1901

The top of the church clock on the east face of the tower is just visible in this picture. It was installed in December 1900 in memory of Sir Robert Samuel Wright's young son Evan Stanley, 'Master Jack,' who died suddenly from 'flu, aged seven. The initials of Sir Robert, his wife Merriel Mabel, their son, and the year in which he died, are painted in the four corners.

See page 109 for more information on Sir Robert.

This postcard was used by Rev W H Laverty to thank well-wishers on the occasion of his Golden Wedding anniversary on 12th June 1922.

Interior of All Saints' Church in 1908

"A magnificent roof of wide span and massive timbers, which sits so grandly upon the Nave walls. It dates from the last quarter of the 14th century, and its great width (about 26ft) is quite exceptional in a Parish Church. Its tie-beams, king-posts and wall-plates are all heavily moulded, and the braced collar and rafter construction is very massive. On one king-post near the west end is carved the head of a man—possibly meant for the master-carpenter, who took an affectionate pride in his work". — *P.M. Johnston, F.S.A.*

The chancel screen was erected in 1892 in memory of Major-General Woodbine Parish CB who died at *The Oaks* in April 1890.

Note the lack of old monuments on the walls—these had been removed during rebuilding work and were not replaced until 1913.

View of Headley High Street looking north in the 1890s

In 1912, Percy Suter wrote to his fiancée:—*"Thought this might interest you as it is copied from a photo in our possession which was taken over 20 years ago. Mr Gamblen had over a thousand done. Notice how short the trees are by Curtis's shop. Now you cannot see the building as you walk down the road. Where the pea sticks are on the right hand corner Kennett's shop now stands. Our place seems the only thing not altered. Same old ivy, same old trees, same old everything."*

He lived in *Suters*, which is the tile-hung house centre-left and is one of the oldest buildings in the parish.

View of Headley High Street looking north 1901

Taken about ten years after the picture on the previous page—the trees have already grown to obscure Curtis's. Note also the growth of ivy and the appearance of the clock on the church tower.

Other useful clues to dating pictures of the High Street are the size of the chestnut tree and the style of the signpost on the triangle. Here the tree, planted in September 1891 on the site of the old stocks, is about 10 years old. The column of the wooden signpost appears to be used as a village notice board!

View of Headley High Street looking north c.1906

The wooden signpost on the triangle has been replaced by a metal one—perhaps not so convenient for bill stickers.

Found on the reverse of the postcard opposite was part of a longer piece of correspondence. It was undated, but presumably written during the First World War:— *"Snow here yesterday and has been very cold. It is just coming on to rain as I write this. I am writing this in the Congregational School Room at Headley where we are working. It is turned into a soldiers club. I am sending you some views of the place. It is a very pretty place. Do you remember Matthew gave me a book I was very interested in called White's Selborne, well ...."* And at that point our imagination must take over.

The chestnut tree in bloom
just before the Second World War

View of Headley High Street looking north, probably 1950s

The signpost is still the lower, metal construction with the 'polo mint' top, but B3002 is now in black letters on a white background, as it has been in more recent years. The picture was probably taken in the 1950s — the card was posted in 1958.

Opposite:—
Bearing a postmark of 20th December 1940, this picture by R.G. Waller of Bordon was presumably taken before the start of hostilities, as the signpost had not been removed. It is now a lower, metal construction with a 'polo mint' top, and the road number B3002 shown in white letters on a dark background below the arms. Note the metal seat around the base of the trunk—also the painted kerbstones.

View of Headley High Street looking south c.1906

Taken probably at the same time as the picture on page 21, but looking south. The photographer seems to be well observed: by the two children outside the *Headley Insurance & House Agency*; by the gentleman in shirtsleeves at the door of Mr Kennett's shop; and in the distance, beyond the *Holly Bush* pub, by a man in an apron outside Mr Rogers' shop.

Behind the triangle, the white stable-block was regarded even in those days as a traffic hazard. It was demolished in 1927—see the picture opposite.

Wakeford's, for many years a butcher's shop, is partly obscured by the chestnut tree.

View of Headley High Street looking south in 1927

Much the same picture as on the previous page, though from a position including part of *The White House* to the left and Curtis's shop by the church gate to the right. A shower seems to have cleared the street on what is obviously a winter's day.

The three wooden buildings with corrugated iron roofs in their time housed a variety of businesses. Mr Kennet was a watchmaker, jeweller and photographer; Mr Louch a harness-maker; and the middle one was for a while a house-agency. *The White House* has, in its time, been a dairy, three small shops, and (as now) a private house.

The Holly Bush and Rogers' stores in 1911

The landlord of the *Holly Bush* at this time was Thomas Keeping. The pub had been sold by Hall of Alton to the larger firm of Messrs Courage in December 1903.

It seems that the *Holly Bush* was not always in this location. Village legend places it across the road in the Wakeford's building—possibly in the left half, with a shop in the right half (see opposite)—when William Cobbett visited Headley on one of his *Rural Rides* in November 1822. The end of a wooden beam on which the inn sign is supposed to have hung is still visible on the north-east corner of Wakeford's.

We believe that the licence moved to its present site at some time prior to 1851 and that the building has been enlarged since then.

View of the Holly Bush Inn, Rogers' Stores and Wakeford's taken in 1931

By 1931, the road has been paved, kerbs added, and the old signpost painted with regulation black and white bands. The buildings look much the same as they did in the 1900s.

A delivery van of the period waits outside the *Holly Bush*. Rogers' stores is the white building across the road with *The Laburnums*, the home of Mr Rogers, to its left. Wakeford's the butchers is to the right.

Rogers' stores in the 1950s

This picture was taken just before Leonard Rogers sold out to Miss Biddy Bargrave Deane for £2,000 in 1957. It had not altered significantly, however, for many years before that.

In 1908, he had inherited the shop from his father William, who had run a business there since 1865. William Rogers used to publish a regular threepenny booklet called the *Headley & Kingsley Almanac and Directory*, full of local information and advertisements.

Some years earlier, in 1830, the stores were run by John Lickfold, who gave an eye-witness account of the agricultural riots of that year in Headley (see page 60).

Wakeford the butcher showing his wares at Christmas around 1901

Frederick Wakeford and his second son James, aged 15, stand in front of their butcher's shop at the turn of the century.

Frederick was one of the three men who planted the chestnut tree in 1891. The others were the Rector, Mr W.H. Laverty, and the licensee of the *Holly Bush* at the time, Mr J Kenyon.

Note the blanked out upper windows. The one in the middle at the front was never a proper window, but two of those at the side are today glazed again.

The War Memorial in 1925, designed by Woodbine Hinchcliffe and unveiled on 4th July 1920 by Major General WD Brownlow, CB—here seen in its original roadside location.

After suffering damage by a Canadian army vehicle during the second world war it was moved in 1945 to its present position, set 10ft further back away from the road.

The 96 officers and men listed 1914–1919 are:— CW Adams, JH Allden, AT Allen, WJ Amor, WP Berry, H Betteridge, H Blackman, S Blake, EK Budd, H Budd, W Budd, GW Bullock, J Caine, WJ Caine, B Cannon, HE Chandler, WA Chisnall, G Christie, W Cole, H Coombes, C Curtis, G Dalton, HR Denney, TJ Denyer, W Dowler, F Duke, C Earl, J Earl, T Earl, FG Elkins, F Fisher, FE Fullick, AA Gamblen, AH Gardiner, W Gardiner, WJ Gates, F Glaysher, S Glaysher, WH Godsmark, HE Goodyear, S Gordon, HE Hack, ESJ Harris, Viscount Hawarden, E Hayter, H Hurlock, WJ Hurlock, FCG Kemball, F Kemp, A Kent, A Larby, A Mackenzie, M Mackenzie, R Mahoney, AC Marshall, WG Marshall, G Mason, J Matthews, CAW McAndrew, F Mileham, CJ Moss, ET Munday, AT Munden, H Newland, WJ North, GV Osborne, JP Phillimore, JL Platt, LV Quennell, R Ramsden, EJ Read, AW Reid, AH Rogers, HE Rogers, WD Rustell, JME Shepherd, W Shrubb, EA Silvester, F Stacey, G Stacey, E Stokes-Roberts, PL Sulman, JS Swan, G Symons, J Ticknor, A Trigg, WJ Tuckey, CA Turner, BJ Viney, PG Viney, J White, FH Whiting, SH Wilson, AC Windibank, RJ Wishart, A Woodger

Headley Church and Rectory in 1931

The front of the old Rectory (above) taken from the Rectory Field, where the current Church Centre and Rectory now stand.

The back of the old Rectory, taken in the 1920s.

The extension on the left was added by Mr Ballantine Dykes (Rector 1848–1872), who said he intended to have a large family. It was taken down in 1965.

Pond in front of the Tithe Barn, c.1903

The Tithe Barn is out of shot to the right of the picture. The Rectory can be seen in the background, behind the smaller building.

A valuation of 1783 describes the Rectory as: *"A very good house, consisting of two parlours and hall, a kitchen and pantry on the ground floor; four bed-chambers, six garrets, four underground cellars, with a brew-house, milk-house, and other convenient offices; also of two spacious barns, a stable, cow-pens, granary, waggon-house, fuel-house, ash-house, etc. The gardens, yard and rick-yard amount to about one and three-quarter acres."*

Loading at the Tithe Barn, c.1903

A tithe barn was originally used to store the tenth of their produce that the farmers had to pay to the Rector as part of his stipend. After payment in kind was commuted to money, the barn was used for storage and market gardening purposes.

Sold in 1965, along with the kitchen garden behind it, to raise money for the modernisation of the rectory, the Tithe Barn has now been sympathetically converted into a dwelling house.

There is a stone let into the wall over what was the stable door, with the date 1680 and the letters S.W.M. These are thought to be the initials of William and Mary Sympson. He was Rector from 1673 to 1695.

We have a record of the names of the rectors of Headley going back to the year 1314, when Walter de Brolnesbourne was presented with the living by the Priory of Merton, replacing one Geoffrey de Hoville.

Among other rectors of the parish:—

- Dr George Holme, 1718–1765, endowed the village with its school in 1755.
- Robert Dickinson—'a jolly big old farmer who suffered from ill-health'—was mobbed by rioters in 1830.
- Wallis Hay Laverty has been our longest-serving rector, holding the office for 56 years from 1872 until his death in December 1928.

Looking down Long Cross Hill from its junction with Curtis Lane—c.1900

Various members of the Gamblen family lived on Long Cross Hill at this time, from *Ivy Bank* down to *Long Cross Farm*.

The Rectory Field is behind the hedge on the right (see next picture). In 1987 the parishioners of Headley staged a successful march through London to deliver a petition to the Archbishop of Canterbury against plans by the Diocese of Guildford to sell the 10-acre site for housing development.

Cows grazing on the Rectory Field by Long Cross Hill—c.1908

On Long Cross Hill, across the road from the field, we can see *Ivy Bank* (redeveloped 2003) and the side of the Post Office. The Congregational Chapel to its right is partly hidden by a tree, and the Manse to its right (with the white gate) borders onto the 'Brae' footpath to Arford Road. This name was given to the footpath by the American author Brett Harte when he stayed at Arford House.

The cows almost certainly belonged to the Gamblen family, who ran a milk round from Long Cross Farm at this time.

Posted on 18th October 1908 at Liphook, this card was sent by an aunt to her nephew in Laverstoke saying "I hope you will like this pc. for your album."

Post Office in Long Cross Hill from the Chapel gate—1908

This picture and the one on the opposite page show Long Cross Hill between Headley High Street (uphill to the left) and Arford (downhill to the right).

William Gamblen (1856–1942) was Postmaster here for more than 60 years—also Parish Clerk for 45 years and a chorister at All Saints for 75 years. After he died, his daughter, Ethel Carter, carried on the business. There was also a Bank here, entered by the door on the left.

Around 1956 the Post Office moved from here to Church Gate House in the High Street, until closing there in March 2002.

Long Cross Hill showing Post Office and Congregational Chapel—c.1908

A recreation room ('The Institute') was later added to the Chapel at the far end, and used as a school room. The Chapel was active until after the Second World War, when rising costs forced it to be sold. The chapel was then used as Dr Williamson's surgery until he retired, after which the building was demolished.

Long Cross House can be seen in the distance where the road bends—the words Headley Restaurant being painted on its gable end. Later, its ground floor was a greengrocer's shop run by Sid Tidey and his sister.

Chapel steps, Long Cross Hill

These steps from the road were built to give access to the recreation room at the back of the chapel. The pillars and left-hand wall can still be seen today, though the steps have now been covered up. Frederick Oscar Parfect is the foreman on the right—he was also a well-digger.

The view opposite, of Long Cross Farm, was taken from a high position to the left of this picture.

Long Cross Farm from the Chapel—c.1908

Long Cross Farm is reputedly haunted by a very benevolent spirit.

During the Second World War it was requisitioned to house officers of the Canadian Army, and Bob Grant of the Fort Garry Horse regiment tells us that they kept their beer supply cool at the bottom of the well. One day the pail tipped over and they lost two dozen very scarce and precious bottles. In trying to retrieve them, he ended up in the water himself. What really hurt, he says, was that the South Alberta Regiment which came to Headley a short time later successfully recovered the beer.

View looking east over Arford from Curtis Hill—c.1903

Long Cross Hill is in the foreground. *Little Barn* cottage is the nearest building, with Lickfold's house (now demolished) behind it, and Kellick's shop (later Bellinger's, now privately owned as *Old Stores*) just visible across Arford Road. To the right is the small wooden building which was Lickfold's garage. Miss Stenning's general shop was built onto the front of the barn next door to Lickfold's—behind the shop there was a large store room which gave access to the barn (now also demolished).

Next to the right are Fern Cottages, and on the far right three cottages which were demolished in the 1950s. Across the road from Fern Cottages at one time was North's the builders in what had previously been a fish and chip shop.

[Thanks to Nic Greene for some of the above information]

On the skyline is *Fairview Terrace*, to the right of it *Burretts* and *Mount Pleasant* which are at the west end of Arford Common. To their right are houses situated on Parish House Bottom (now Beech Hill Road), and on the extreme right is the house now called *Brook Lodge*, on Bowcott Hill.

View looking west over Arford from Beech Hill Road—c1903

A view in the opposite direction, taken from the point where smoke appears to be rising in the previous picture. Tracks from Arford Common on the right here join Parish House Bottom (later renamed Beech Hill Road, due to incomers' sensibilities about bottoms!).

Like many of the pictures from this period, tree growth would now make this view impossible to see. To the right is *Shingle Cottage* with *The Orchard* just visible behind it. To the left is *Rock Cottage*, then *Alpha Cottage* and *Greensleeves*. In the distance are houses on Bowcott Hill.

Tidey's bakery and The Crown in Arford—1931

Originally the Post Office before this moved to Long Cross Hill, the shop was then run as a bakery by Robert Tidey until after the Second World War, then by the Amey family.

The *Crown* building is said to date from the latter years of the 17th century when it bore the sign of *The Duke of Richmond's Arms*. In 1876, James Upperton sold the property to C.H. Master for £1,000. Mr Master subsequently became the first chairman of Friary Holroyd & Healey's Breweries of Guildford—and the *Crown* still serves Friary Meux beer to this day.

Road junction in Arford—left: Lickfold's Garage; right: Bellinger's Stores—pre-1915

Two Lickfold brothers and their wives ran the Garage and single hand-operated petrol pump next door. Eventually the brothers built a much larger garage in Crabtree Lane (now known as *Tonard's*), but the petrol pump still remained, and little Cecily Lickfold braved all weathers, at any time of day, to answer the toot of a horn. The shop was then run by Miss Stenning, whose brother was a baker, selling bread, cakes, confectionery, cigarettes, haberdashery, toys and news-papers.

On the back of this card is the message:— *"Quiet time, done nothing to-day except eat. I could stick this a lifetime, but it will hardly be always like this. We have received our mobilization, boots & other equipment. I hope Elsie & you and all at home are well, as this leaves me the same at present. Your own Fred."* —Posted 13th September 1915 to Mrs Cullough in Co. Down.

Mrs Chuck outside Corner House at the road junction in Arford

The wooden buildings to the left have been part of a builder's yard for at least a hundred years. At one time they were owned by Henry Knight (1805–1903) who, as a boy of ten, remembered standing outside the *Royal Anchor* at Liphook watching the prisoners from the Battle of Waterloo. It was he who climbed on the roof of the Church when it caught fire in 1836, trying to put out the flames. By 1901, he owned 40 properties in the village.

The next builder to live here was Mr H.R. Chuck, also an undertaker and for very many years a churchwarden. This is thought to be a picture of his wife. He was followed by the Collings family, and then Robert Moodie who had his upholstery workshop there until a few years ago.

Outside Eashing Cottages, Arford Road—after 1912

This undated picture is from a more peaceful time than would be allowed today, with the current use of Arford as a commuter rat-run for fast cars.

Eashing Cottages were built around 1912 as a speculative venture by a Mr Peachey of Eashing Farm near Godalming. They look much the same today. In the background is Bohanna's shop. Between them runs the Arford stream.

During and after the Second World War, this area of Arford was severely flooded by rain flowing off Ludshott Common which was denuded of vegetation after being used as a tank training ground.

The tanks themselves were also driven through Arford's narrow lanes regularly on their way to manoeuvres, causing severe damage to property here at times.

The Wheatsheaf—c.1908

The Inclosure Award map of 1855 shows *The Wheatsheaf* in this location, though whether it is the same building is debatable. The flat-roofed extension now houses the public bar, with steps on the right (enclosed in recent years) leading up to the lounge bar at a higher level.

An earlier publican here was John Lickfold (see page 28)—Mr Laverty says he came to the *Wheatsheaf* in 1835, then moved on to run Headley Mill in 1845.

Village legend says that Eade's stonemason's yard was here, possibly before the pub, and that it made one of the two 'Sailor's Stones' erected on Hindhead Common around 1826. Certainly the old map shows the field behind to be called Arford Stone Field. The 1851 census gives three mason's labourers living in Arford, but no stonemason.

The *Wheatsheaf* was demolished and the site redeveloped in 2002.

Junction at bottom of Barley Mow Hill

The previous picture was taken from a position by the white gate. The *Wheatsheaf* is now slightly behind us on the left—the road ahead is The Hanger leading to Frensham Lane—a gate leads to *The Oaks* (see page 49)—the main road bends right, up Barley Mow Hill towards Churt.

To the left along The Hanger is the site of a sheep wash. Two shearers at a time were given the privilege of using this, the last two being James Marshall of Parish House Bottom, and the father of George Glaysher of Barford. Further on beyond the sheep wash there were watercress beds.

In 1806 an agreement was drawn up between Edward Benham and John Willoughby to settle a dispute over the use of the water downstream from here.

View over The Wheatsheaf and up Barley Mow Hill

Another view of the junction on the previous page. The large white house facing us was one of several shops in Arford at the time. According to Mr Laverty: "Bohanna took Curtis' shop at Arford—good voice, choir." He was also a coal merchant. The building had in the past been used as a Quaker Meeting House.

The first white house facing us further up the hill is *The Birches* built for James Allden, who married Henry Knight's daughter. Behind that to one side is *Sunnybank*, and on the skyline directly behind is *Hillborough* which Mr Beck (see the Introduction) built for his retirement.

Just visible among the trees up Barley Mow Hill to the left are *Brontë Cottage* and *Hillside*, the latter now known as *Little Barley Mow*. A track known as 'The Shambles' leads up to Hearn from the bottom of Barley Mow Hill behind these houses—we assume from the name that animals were slaughtered there at one time.

'The Oaks'—before the First World War

Lord Robert Cecil M.P., became Viscount Cranborne in 1865 while listed as a resident here. He later became third Marquis of Salisbury in 1868, and then prime minister both in 1885 and again during the Boer War.

Major-General Woodbine Parish lived here until 1890, and Archdeacon Norris wrote his account of the parish church while staying here in 1903.

The house was demolished during redevelopment in 2002.

'Hillside' on Barley Mow Hill

Now known as *Little Barley Mow*, the house has been altered, extended and painted pink on the outside since this picture was taken.

During the Second World War, camouflaged tanks were parked up Barley Mow Hill and Nissen huts erected in the front gardens. And local girls remember darning the socks of Canadian soldiers billeted near here for a packet of chewing gum.

Fellmongers Cottage at bottom of Beech Hill Road—c.1900s

Another undated picture. Fellmongers prepared skins for a tanner, and there used to be a tanyard opposite this property where *Brookside Cottage* is now. Mr Laverty in his parish notes says that the father of James Mills was the last fellmonger to live here. James died in March 1898 aged 82. Mr Laverty had earlier (in the 1870s) called the property 'Rotten Row' because of its tumble-down condition!

The Arford stream runs close by, and used to cross the road by a ford not far from where this picture is taken. The stream also supplied the tanyard.

'Arford Spring Cottage'

Now known as *Ivy Cottage* at the bottom of Bowcott Hill, an area once known as Parfect's Hollow. The Arford stream runs through the field in front of a stone wall which borders the footpath (No.30) along Fullers Vale. People can still remember collecting their water from the spring which came out of a pipe in a wall by the house.

As 'Arford Lodge' in the 1900s

From an essay on Headley by Mrs WE Belcher in 1925: *"There are several little beauty spots [in Headley parish], such as the winding piece of road at the bottom of Parfect's Hollow by Arford spring and pond..."*

In the 1900s the house was referred to as 'Arford Lodge' according to Cherry Forray whose grandmother 'Hartie' Harnett was born there in 1879.

A Cottage, Headley.

The cottage in the picture above is thought to be Yew Tree Cottage on Arford Common, shown in a later picture on the right.

According to Dolly McGhee, who knew it well, a Mrs Parfitt lived there. She says the left hand door led to the washhouse, and she thinks the building lost its thatch just after the Second World War.

Yew Tree Cottage, Arford Common

Laurel Cottage, Bowcott Hill—1950s

Laurel Cottage is typical of a number of dwellings in and around Headley which started life as 'squatters cottages'.

"These were erected during the night, trees cut down to form the framework, the walls being made of turf and the roof thatched with heather. Before morning wives and children were installed—if the squatter had no children of his own he borrowed some, as the law would not allow the bailiffs to remove the roof of a house containing children. On being thus occupied for a certain time the cabin and land on which it stood could be claimed."— Mrs W.E. Belcher, 1925.

This view, taken in the 1950s, looks north from Headley Hill Road over Beech Hill Road to Arford Common. The house behind is probably *Mount Pleasant*.

The Pines, Headley—1897

This has been identified as Headley Hill Road. According to Elsie Johnson it was still known as 'The Pines' in her lifetime and looked as it does in the picture.

'Pinehurst'—built 1899; later renamed 'Benifold'

Across the road from *Laurel Cottage*, but miles apart in terms of refinement, *Pinehurst* was built on Headley Hill in 1899 for Edward Frinneby Hubbuck.

Pine Cottage sits in Fullers Vale close to where 'Breakneck Hill' footpath (No.29) climbs to Bowcott Hill.

'Pine Cottage' in Fullers Vale with 'Pinehurst' above

'Benifold' when it became an Ecumenical House of Prayer

At some undetermined time, the house name changed from *Pinehurst* to *Benifold*.

Described in their brochure as "a 20-roomed house with eight acres of grounds," *Benifold* was from 1963–1970 an Ecumenical House of prayer where 'people of all sorts and ages' were welcome. Initially the organisation also owned *Little Benifold*, just across the road, using this as a Warden's house, but it was later sold separately.

Then followed a significant culture shift, as the pop group Fleetwood Mac moved in. The group made four albums during their time here, and it is said that on the second floor there are still some paintings on the wall reminiscent of Christine McVie's artwork for the cover of the 'Kiln House' album.

They eventually left for California in late 1974 to achieve world-wide success. In the village, they are remembered by regulars down at the *Wheatsheaf*.

'Hilland' before extension—c.1890

Hilland Farm was owned by the Collins family in the 1841 & 1851 censuses—and by the Bridger family in 1881 (when the farm was 140 acres, employing two men and two boys).

Walter Phillips bought the estate in 1889, and extended the house before getting married in 1894. He was Rector's Warden for 40 years, a JP and a school manager. He died in 1937, being remembered now in the names of Phillips Close and Phillips Crescent, built on part of the old estate.

During the Second World War and into the 1950s the estate was owned by the Thomson-Glover family. It was later sold for property development, and the house and its outbuildings demolished. Some parts of the building are known to have been re-used in other local properties.

'Hilland' after extension

Hilland and Pinehurst, Headley.

'Pinehurst' (distant right) viewed from Hilland Farm—1908

Headley Grange was the workhouse until 1870

This building was purpose-built in 1795 as the 'House of Industry' for the parishes of Headley, Bramshott and Kingsley at a cost of some £1,500, to shelter their infirm, aged paupers, and orphan or illegitimate children.

In November 1830 it was sacked by a mob of several hundred people, many coming from neighbouring parishes, during the so-called agricultural 'Swing' riots. For this, seven men were sentenced to transportation to Australia.

It continued to be used as a workhouse until sold in 1870 to a builder, who converted it into a private house now known as *Headley Grange*.

During the 1970s it was let out to various recording artists, who found the acoustics suitable for use as a recording venue. Most famously, Led Zeppelin recorded their world-wide hit *Stairway to Heaven* here in 1971.

Grange Lane, Headley.

Grange Lane in 1908, now Liphook Road

A view from the Village Green looking down Liphook Road towards *Headley Grange*. Hilland Farm is behind the hedge on the left.

The writer of this card was in a poetic frame of mind—the message on the back reads: *"Dos't remember yon road? So many thanks for having my hubby on Friday—he much enjoyed himself. 'Tis lovely down here. Am returning on Thursday."* She also notes: *"Crab Tree House fence on right."*

That *Crab Tree House* is now called *Yeoman's Place*, and Rogers' old shop (see page 28) is now called *Crabtree House*—such is the confusion of history.

View across the Village Green and Rectory Field to the Church and Rectory in 1925. The Holme School with flagstaff is on the left.

Headley Summer Fete,
WEDNESDAY, JUNE 29th, 1904,
(Under the management of the Rev. W. H. Laverty; any profit or loss falling to the Vestry Fund.)

By the kind permission of Lieut.-Gen. Sir John French, K.C.B., K.C.M.G., Commanding the 1st Army Corps, and of Lieut.-Col. A. V. Payne, Commanding the Regiment.

MILITARY SPORTS
By the Non-Commissioned Officers and Men of
THE WILTSHIRE REGIMENT.

THE BAND of the Regiment will play during the Afternoon.

CHILDREN'S MUSICAL DRILL
under the direction of Mr. C. H. Box.

REFRESHMENTS by Mr. Ransom of Farnham.

The Programme of the Sports and the Band Programme are given on the next page.

The village school was founded in 1755 by the then Rector, Dr George Holme, and the building extended several times over the ensuing years. In 1991 it was sold, and school activities transferred to the Openfields site behind the church.

The Village Green and Rectory Field have both been used for community activities over the years. Since the Second World War, the field has reverted to agricultural use—but the Green is still the site of visiting fairs, carnivals, car boot sales, open-air services, and many other local events.

Part 2

Headley Down and beyond

HEADLEY DOWN AND BEYOND

Going east from the centres of Headley and Arford, the ground rises to an area of heathland.

This was called Headley Down on maps even as early as 1801, and Mr Laverty had also proposed it in 1913, but the name was not formalised for the area until the post office announced in March 1923 that 'the official name of the Telephone Call Office which has been established on Stone Hill will be Headley Down.'

In earlier days it was relatively unpopulated due to the poor nature of its soil, but from about the 1870s onwards, a fashion developed in favour of the healthy air which this high ground was supposed to offer. Houses began to appear on the estates there known as Beech Hill and Stone Hill, and, to the extreme east of the parish, the rapid development of Hindhead as a notable health resort promoted the growth of Grayshott village in its wake.

By the end of the 19th century, Grayshott had become so dissimilar from its mother village that it was decided to create a separate parish there, centred round the new church of St Luke's.

In our tour of the eastern parts of the parish, we shall visit the 'new' buildings on Headley Down, and the open expanses of Ludshott Common which, although a natural 'playground' for Headley residents, in fact lies almost totally in Bramshott parish.

Then, following the old parish boundary, we pass by the top of Waggoners Wells, go through Grayshott, and along the line of the county boundary with Surrey down Whitmore Vale, ending up in Barford.

But first, we stop at a once-lost beauty spot in Fullers Vale …

Fullers Vale pond, before the First World War

The pond is fed by natural springs. Note the horse and cart waiting in Pond Road.

Even as late as in the 1891 census, Fullers Vale was still referred to as Fullers Bottom—but late-Victorian sensibilities ensured that most of our local bottoms were transformed into vales!

Fullers Vale pond — 1931

Taken from the opposite direction compared with the picture on the previous page, we see the junction of Fullers Vale and Beech Hill with the corner shop which for many years was run by Mrs Pearce. Reflected in the water is *Fernvale*.

This card was actually posted during the Second World War, in August 1942.

The pond was drained in 1972 after a series of floodings had affected Arford, lower down the valley. Metal railings were put along the roadside, and the pond bed left untouched to fill up gradually with vegetation and inevitable litter.

Finally in 2003 a restoration project began to clear the site of the debris of thirty years' neglect and bring the pond back to its previous glory.

An interesting event at Fullers Vale pond

This picture is undated, but looks to be taken in the 1920s. Presumably the driver had misjudged the bend, as has happened to many others since.

Elsie Johnson (neé Pearce) remembers the occasion well. The car in the pond was on its way home from a New Year's party at *Hilland*. She lived in the shop across the road, and says that her father was called out in the middle of the night to help get some girls out. The year was sometime between 1922 and 1924 she thinks. She is not in the picture herself.

During the Second World War, a tank coming down Fullers Vale hit the letter box at the bottom of the Kenton House drive, by the brick pillar—the box was subsequently moved to the other side of Pond Road, where it is now.

Bottom of Beech Hill, probably circa 1904

Taken, we assume, from *Kenton House*. In the foreground is *The Haven*. Across the road are *Fernvale* and *Oakdene* with ornamental gardens, not long after they were built by J.H. Viney Jnr in the 1890s. Beyond them is Ferndale Terrace, and to their left near the corner of Fullers Vale is the shop.

On the other side of Fullers Vale, what was then largely clear farmland on the hill top has today become the upper end of the Hilland housing estate.

Honeysuckle Lane—1924

Honeysuckle Lane leads from Beech Hill to Kenley Road. A certain amount of development had already occurred on other parts of Headley Down when this picture was taken—see following pages—but had not spread here yet.

The message on the back, written in August 1928, says: *"Have arrived here – are now going to have our bread and cheese in a field. This is typical of all our walks, but the colouring is exquisite."*

Wilsons Road, Headley Down—1912

Taken from a vantage point on Linden Road, the nearest house is *Stonehill Cottage*, just at the top of the steep hill on Wilsons Road. Further up on the opposite side of the road is Wilson's shop, which can be identified by the overhang on its right side above the shop window. Crossing at this point is Fairview Road. In the background we see *The Boreen*, demolished in more recent years and the site developed into a close of smaller properties.

Posted in August 1915: *"I am still holding on – very nasty at times – horrid old thing. Never mind, just over another week and then goodbye to her – thank goodness. Have put a little mark where our house is – you can just see the chimney of it."*

Kenley Road and Fairview Road, Headley Down—c.1910

Taken from much the same viewpoint as the previous picture, and probably at around the same time. The houses shown here have been identified as follows:—

Fairview Road (higher): Ringmore Villas, Cherry Tree Cottage, High Pines
Kenley Road (lower): Kenley House, Heatherley

All these buildings are still standing today, although the growth of vegetation and further housing development since that time now make this view an impossibility.

Bungalows at Stonehill, Headley Down—c.1912

The name Stonehill here, as on the previous page, referred at the time to this area of Headley Down generally rather than to any particular part of it. This picture shows the junction of Fairview Road (left) with Carlton Road (right).

Houses have been identified by Dolly McGhee as (left to right): Stanton, Pine Trees, The Beehive, Hazeldene, Heathlands.

Dolly worked at Hazeldene for Giles Henry Zeal and his family, who were associated with Zeal thermometers and Whitefriers glass.

Posted in October 1913, and addressed from The Boreen, the author of the postcard above writes: *"This is the little hamlet near where our house is situated ... I like the country so far very much."*

View towards 'Stonedene', Headley Down—1912

The house in view here is actually *Woodlands*, situated at the end of Pond Road. *Stonedene* itself, a somewhat larger house, can just be seen in the distance below the overhanging tree bough.

During the Second World War, the King of Norway lived at *Stonedene* after his country was invaded by the Germans.

The house has since been demolished, and in its place is the development called Stonedene Close.

Carlton Road, Headley Down—c.1910

Of the same date as the pictures of Kenley Road (p.71) and Grayshott Road (p.78), we are looking up Carlton Road towards its junction with Grayshott Road.

Carlton Road had been developed as far as its junction with Fairview Road. We can see *Primrose Glen* with *Little Orchard* behind it. The houses to the right are along Seymour Road, with *Heathcroft* identifiable by its gables.

We believe that one of the girls in the picture became Mrs Dangerfield.

Post Office, Carlton Road

A later picture. Situated near the junction of Carlton Road and the main Grayshott Road, this temporary building served Headley Down as its post office after Wilson's shop closed in the 1960s. It was built in the front garden of *Down End*.

The post office moved in 1974 to its present site at Whittle's store in Eddey's Lane, and this building was demolished.

The Land of Nod is the name given to an estate lying between Headley Down and Barford (see also the map on page 80).

According to the present owner, the name came about when a man called Cane (or Keyne) who had been excommunicated lived here, we think in the early 1700s.

In the Bible, it was the land to which Cain was exiled after he had slain Abel.

Pine and heather at the Land of Nod—1912

It is unclear exactly where this picture was taken—possibly at the point on footpath No.19 where it descends sharply to the present parish boundary with Grayshott.

However, many people can still remember the area where Heatherlands has now been built as once being like this, 'the prettiest spot in Headley' from which there were wonderful views.

Ludshott Common—1917

Ludshott Common has belonged to The National Trust since 1908. Along with similar properties in Surrey and West Sussex it forms part of an extensive area of 'lowland heathland' owned by the Trust in this region. Continual management of the property has ensured, not only that the panoramic views of the South Downs and East Hampshire Hangers shown in this picture remain with us today, but also that the Common supports a diversity of rare animals and plants.

However, during two World Wars it was given over to the Army for training purposes, and significantly in the Second World War was used as a tank training ground. Locals remember it then as 'just a sea of mud' and 'absolutely barren of vegetation except for the bigger trees.'

By the road from Grayshott, looking towards Headley Down—c.1910

Two ladies relax on a bench at the edge of Ludshott Common. In the background we can see *Wits End* at the junction of Seymour Road and Grayshott Road.

This view shows the small section of the common that is actually in Headley parish. The boundary with Bramshott runs from about this point diagonally left towards the back of properties in Furze Hill Road. This triangular piece of 'Headley Common' was given to The National Trust by Ingham Alexander Whitaker in 1911 to commemorate the Coronation of George V.

The road, known locally as the 'Grayshott Straight' and now designated B3002, runs between Hindhead and Bordon. During the Second World War, army tanks were hidden under the trees to the right, crossing the road for their crews to practice military operations on the common.

Ludshott Common—1915

Probably taken a little further towards Grayshott along the same road.

Until the early part of the 20th century, the commons were grazed by a variety of different animals which cropped the vegetation and restricted the growth of tree saplings. Since then, this maintenance has had to be performed by man.

The National Trust is carrying out plans to restore endangered species to their natural habitat—these include birds such as the nightjar, woodlark and Dartford warbler and reptiles such as the sand lizard and the smooth snake.

Map of the Wishanger Manor Estate—c.1868

The estate, extending from Grayshott to Frensham Great Pond and over the county boundary into parts of Surrey in places, is shown shaded.

Note in particular the absence of buildings in Grayshott and Hindhead at this time.

Front of Grayshott Hall—1882

Described in 1882 as a 'small mansion erected within the past five years,' and pictured here before the extensions of 1887 which added a tower and other features.

In the 1860s it was even smaller, being then called Grayshott Farm and described as a 'two-storeyed stone and brick house with small low rooms, windows with diamond panes and doors with bolts and bars'. It was here in 1867 that Alfred Tennyson and his family rented rooms for about a year.

Joseph Whitaker of Palermo bought the Wishanger Estate in 1884 for one of his sons, Alexander Ingham Whitaker, who lived here until 1927.

More recently it has become a Health Fitness Retreat, for which Whitaker's motto in Latin over his front door seems entirely appropriate: *Pax Intrantibus* on entering—*Salus Exeuntibus* on leaving.

The lane down to Waggoners Wells from Headley Road—1907

Here we are looking down the line of the boundary between Bramshott parish (on the right) and part of the old Headley parish, now Grayshott (on the left). The lane leads to the ford at Waggoners Wells top pond, and in past times was used as a pack-horse route between Haslemere and Frensham.

Written on the back of this card, posted in September 1907 at Shottermill: *"A view in our lane! The cottages are a little higher up than where I have put mark"*—but the mark seems to have disappeared, so we are not quite sure to which cottages the writer was referring.

It is interesting to note that a similar postcard was also available at the time without the boy included!

One of the ponds in Stoney Bottom—1899

An unusual shot—entitled 'Waggoners Wells,' it in fact shows one of the smaller and lesser-known ponds higher up the valley. Again, we are looking along the old parish boundary, this time up Stoney Bottom towards Grayshott. The building just visible in the distance is probably the Cenacle convent, demolished in 1999.

At the time the picture was taken, Flora Thompson would have walked this way on the Sunday rambles she describes in 'Heatherley.'

Near the head of the 'bottom' (one of the few to have retained this title locally) is a stone, marking the junction of this boundary with Surrey.

County Boundary stone
in Crossways Road, Grayshott
H = Headley; S F = Surrey/Frensham

Crossways Road, Grayshott—c.1900

Thomas Wright wrote in 1898: *"Grayshott looks like a doll's village, not so much because of the size of the houses, but because of their quaintness ... they are all new, having been erected during the last five or six years."*

On the right we see Walter Chapman's post office in which Flora Thompson was working as Sub-Office Assistant. In Jubilee Terrace next door are Prince the baker, Munday the greengrocer, and an off-licence run first by Upex and then Milton. Behind the tree is Deas the grocer's.

On the left is Victoria Terrace where 'Madame' Fanny Warr occupied four shops with her various businesses which, according to Flora Thompson, were advertised on the board as: *Milliner and Costumier, Baby Linen and Real Lace, Lending Library (frequent boxes from Mudie's), Stationery and Artists' Materials.*

Bowes Cottage, Whitmore Vale—1917

Beware of captions on cards! This is a view of Bowes Cottage, on the Hampshire side of Whitmore Vale, and not of Whitmore Vale Farm itself which is in Surrey.

From Crossways Road, in the previous picture, we travel over the 'Fiveways' crossroads and along Whitmore Vale Road. The road soon drops past Bowes Cottage to enter a narrow valley. The old parish boundary of Headley encompassed Grayshott and then ran along this valley, following the county boundary and the stream bed all the way to Frensham Great Pond. Headley's neighbouring parish in Surrey for many years was Frensham, until 1865, when Churt gained the status of being a parish in its own right.

Interestingly, the name of the valley is spelt Whitmore in Hampshire, but Whitmoor in Surrey.

Mill pond at Barford middle mill—1906

There were once three mills operating on the Barford stream, the upper and lower ones involved in paper-making, while the middle one ground corn. The county and parish boundaries run down the centre of the stream—so while the Lower Mill was said in 1884 to have the largest water wheel in Surrey, the mill itself was actually in Hampshire.

Barford middle mill, shown in these pictures, stopped working commercially at some time prior to the 1930s and has now been converted into a private house.

Barford middle mill—1923

The upper and lower mills stopped working in the 1880s and have since been demolished, though the mill house of the lower mill still stands—an impressive three-storey building near Barford bridge.

Tilbury and Warren families were shown as being involved in papermaking at Barford in the 1841 and 1851 censuses of Headley parish, but by 1891 only a flock mill is mentioned.

The middle mill was the oldest-established of the three, being mentioned in a pipe roll of the manor of Farnham in 1264—the others dated only from the 1730s.

The ford at Barford, pre-1900

We are looking from Surrey (Churt) into Hampshire (Headley). Barford Stream Cottage is in the background. The stream has just passed through Barford lower mill, to the left, and is on its way down to Simmonstone.

This card was still being used in 1907, after the ford had been bridged.

Same view after a bridge replaced the ford—1906

Reports in the Farnham, Haslemere & Hindhead Herald:—

23 Dec 1899: Headley Mill ford – the latest stage in agitation for a bridge to replace the dangerous ford has brought the wished-for structure well within the prospect of being built...

26 May 1900: Discussions started about a bridge at Barford, to be three-quarters in Hampshire...

Barford got its bridge within six years—at Headley Mill we are still waiting a century later!

Barford Stream and the path to Simmonstone—1923

The footpath on the right (now Headley footpath No.23) comes down from the junction of Churt Road and Hammer Lane to cross the stream and county boundary by a footbridge. The footpath from Churt (now Frensham footpath No.31) comes out at the stile.

Both then follow the track in the foreground, which leads eventually to Frensham Great Pond.

The remains of the brick shed on the left can still be found in the undergrowth today.

Part 3

Along the Wey

ALONG THE WEY

The southern arm of the River Wey runs through the west of the parish in a loop, flowing from south to north, with various smaller tributaries joining it. In the past there have been a number of water mills along its length—now only Headley Mill remains in working order.

We start our journey in Hollywater, one of the 'forgotten' hamlets of the parish. It sits at the point where three parishes join.

In the old days, the boundaries of Headley, Bramshott and Selborne met opposite the *Royal Oak* pub at the 'centre of a chimney of a house inhabited by a person named Eade'. This house was demolished between 1881 and 1890, leaving no trace as to where the chimney stood. A joint party from Bramshott and Headley in 1890 then determined it to be: *"in a small garden lying due north and 23 paces from the door of the house inhabited by Charles Fisher; the spot being 5 yards from the S. bank, and 7 yards from the W. bank, and 12 paces from a wild cherry tree situated on the E. side of the garden."*

A tributary of the Wey flows through the hamlet from Hollywater Pond, whose water, tradition says, had curative properties.

The bridge at Hollywater—c.1906

We are looking east along Walldown Road to where it is crossed by Hollywater Road. The stream passing under the bridge joins the River Wey near Lindford. Upstream (to the right), it was called the Hollywater Stream; downstream the Deadwater Stream.

In 1929, most of Hollywater was transferred into the new parish of Whitehill. Hollywater Road then became the boundary with Headley.

The message on the back reads: *"Do you know anyone on here? This is our bridge with Nellie and Grace and another little girl."* It was Nellie and Grace Trussler.

The ford at Standford—1901

It is said that the Romans used this ford to cross the River Wey on their march from London to do battle in the west. More surely, the agricultural rioters came in the opposite direction on 23rd November 1830 during their march from Selborne to sack Headley Workhouse.

This ford still exists today, with stony bottom, and declared as 'unfit for vehicles.' The river is bridged for such traffic some fifty yards downstream.

View over Standford—1908

This view was taken from footpath No.32 which comes over from Headley Fields.

The road through the hamlet from Lindford to Liphook (now B3004) can be seen clearly, as can the mill pond for Standford Paper Mill which, at the time, stretched between the ford and the road bridge. The mill itself had been closed for several years by this time, although Bramshott Paper Mill just upstream was still in business.

Beyond can be seen the pub and houses around Standford Green. The buildings in the foreground lie along Tulls Lane. The ford is out of view to the left.

The 'Robin Hood & Little John' in Standford, prior to demolition in the late 1950s

This building stood nearer to the ford than does the current *Robin Hood*—on the site now occupied by the bungalow *Sherwood*.

The landlords are recorded in the Headley censuses and elsewhere as follows— 1861 & 71 William Sutton; 1881 David Frost; 1885 Walter Piggott; 1887 & 1903 George Brown.

Road through Standford—before 1912

This card was posted in May 1912, but the picture is undated. The buildings to the right are Standford Farm and *Eveley*, renamed in 1936.

Standford's two water mills were on this side of the road, one just behind Standford Farm which manufactured paper until the late 1800s, and the other (see next page) opposite *Reynolds* further downstream.

Ahead, the road to Liphook soon bears right to cross the River Wey over the bridge and pass Standford Green, while Tulls Lane continues straight on along the bank of the river.

Standford Corn Mill

These two pages show a pair of mills which operated within a few hundred yards of each other. In fact there were four mills on the short stretch of river, little over a mile long, between Passfield and Lindford.

On this page, taken at an unknown date, is Standford Corn Mill, clearly showing its exposed mill wheel. This has now been removed and the mill building has become a private house, *The Old Corn Mill*.

Headley Mill—circa 1930

Downstream is Headley Mill, which is also a corn mill and is still in commercial operation today.

Here the mill wheel is enclosed—it is behind the right-hand lower small window. Apparently this was not always so, there having once been a gap in which the wheel was exposed between two buildings—the mill house on the right, and the mill on the left.

Headley Mill viewed from across the mill pond—c.1910

Headley Mill, owned by the Ellis family since 1914, is the last water mill working commercially in Hampshire. The mill wheel is breast-shot from a head of seven and a half feet and drives four pairs of old-style stones, each nearly 4ft in diameter and 10ins thick, producing flour and animal feeds.

It is assumed that there has been a mill here since Saxon times. Mr Laverty, when he was Rector of Headley, said that it was mentioned in the Domesday Book—other scholars have disputed this.

The clear view of the mill shown here is no longer to be seen, due to the growth of trees along the border of the road. Note how narrow the mill pond is—it was later widened considerably.

Headley Mill Farm, 1910—now Wey House

This and the picture opposite are taken from much the same spot, and show the Liphook road as it comes from the mill, passes Headley Mill Farm and bends towards us on the way to Standford.

Headley Mill Farm was at one time owned by Sir Archibald Macdonald, with Walter Lickfold working as tenant farmer. It was bought in 1915 by James Branson (see page 114).

The current owner, who is an architect, tells us that the building is based on an original 13th century open hall structure to which many additions and alterations have been made.

Haymaking at Headley Mill—c.1890s

The mill pond now covers the field we see here. The date of the photograph is thought to be in the 1890s. A small drainage ditch can be seen above, crossing the meadow to a sluice near the mill.
The photograph is taken from a position close to a second drain.

In the recent photograph on the right, looking from the mill, we see the bed of the larger mill pond as it is today when given a 'draining'. It clearly shows the line of the ditches in the mud.

The ford at Headley Mill

As mentioned on page 89, there has been talk of bridging this ford since 1899, but a hundred years later traffic is still splashing its way through between Headley and Bordon.

In this picture, at the rear of the mill, we are looking away from Bordon across the Wey towards the junction with Liphook Road. This has been the site of many accidents in the past, and the authorities have now decreed that traffic may enter the ford only from the Headley direction, the return from Bordon being over Lindford or Standford bridges.

Behind us, the road marks the 1929 boundary between the parishes of Headley and Whitehill—land on the Mill side as far as Hollywater Road remains in Headley.

The garage at Lindford

National Benzole Mixture and Shell petrol are for sale at the two manual pumps in this undated picture. Mobiloil is also available.

During the Second World War, Joyce Dickie was cycling on her way from Headley to work at Bordon telephone exchange when an air raid occurred. She remembers: *"I'd just got to Lindford when the planes came over. I was stopped there and had to get down in the pit with the men at the garage."*

A garage was in business here until 1999, when the site was cleared for redevelopment.

The 'Royal Exchange' at Lindford crossroads

The road to Headley bears left at the pub; that to Liphook goes straight ahead. Frensham Lane goes off to the left in front of the shop. This view together with the one of the garage on the opposite page is almost panoramic.

This card was posted in May 1924, although the photograph may be somewhat older than that.

On the back, the writer says: *"I am pleased to say that a Son arrived here this morning. I will write a letter later on."* The word Son was written in pencil—perhaps it needed last minute verification!

Lindford was in Headley parish at this time, becoming part of Whitehill parish when it was first formed in 1929, and later a parish in its own right in 1982.

Bridge over the Wey at Lindford—1901

The slope down to the old ford is still visible to the left of the bridge. Beyond is Oliver's Farm, situated at the southern end of Broxhead Common—today still in Headley parish.

The original road went from here over Broxhead Common to Sleaford and Kingsley —only later was the link made to Bordon.

Nowhere has the battle to save local commons been fought with more determination than on Broxhead. Commoners have in the past challenged both the Army and civilian landowners here with considerable success. At the forefront of this activity was the late John Ellis of Headley Mill.

Oxney Pond—1900

We deviate from our journey along the main course of River Wey to visit another tributary, and part of the original western boundary of Headley parish which went through the middle of Oxney Pond.

Perambulations which 'beat the bounds' of the parish in the 18th and 19th centuries describe the route from Sleaford up the 'Forest stream' and through 'Oxney marsh' to the penstock (or sluice) of 'Ogmoor Great Pond.' (This latter pond was situated where the Council's recycling depot now stands in Station Road, Bordon!)

The various dams, culverts and sluices along this boundary seem to indicate some commercial activity here in the past, perhaps related to iron, but we are left with no positive record as to what or when this might have been.

Headley Park, before 1912

Headley, having been in a detached portion of the Manor of Bishops Sutton, has never had a resident Lord of the Manor, but the various owners of Headley Park have probably been the nearest thing—even though they were technically in the Manor of Broxhead.

On this card, posted in August 1912, Percy Suter wrote to his future mother-in-law: *"Many thanks for the card. Sorry for the delay in answering, but have been so busy getting ready for our Flower Show that it slipped my memory. I entered two things and managed to pull off two first prizes, eight shillings in all. This is the country house of one of our local gentry."*

Another view of Headley Park, when it was a school

The Directory of Headley in 1878 says: *"Headley Park is the property of Sir Henry Keating, but the house was taken down many years ago"*. The original house was situated some distance to the south west of the present building shown on these pages. This was built in 1884 and was, according to a newspaper article of 1904, *"positioned to view the Hindhead hills, but this is now obscured by trees."*

Sir Henry Keating was a celebrated Victorian judge, as was the next owner, Sir Robert Wright. Both resided here for nearly 20 years. Sir Robert died in 1901, and Charles McAndrew who owned a shipping line bought the property in 1904. It is said that he also looked at Sandringham at the time, but chose Headley Park instead.

The McAndrews left during the Second World War—the estate subsequently became a private school, then a club for émigré Lithuanians.

Today it is a hotel.

Looking down Bull's Hollow—c.1906

Bull's Hollow at Picketts Hill is one of several good local examples of a sunken lane. The road leads down to the River Wey at Brockford Bridge, then passes Headley Park on its way to Sleaford.

Out of view, behind us at the top of the bank to the left, the remains of a lime kiln still exist today (see small picture).

Remains of lime kiln above Bull's Hollow

Heath Hill, near Dockenfield—1904

This road is a continuation of the one shown crossing the River Wey and passing Mellow Farm on the next page. Here it climbs past the sand quarry, negotiates a blind right-hand bend at the top, and soon crosses over the present county boundary into Surrey not far from the old convent in Dockenfield.

Sand from the quarry used to be used by the Farnham Pottery at Wrecclesham.

Lower House Farm—1904 (now called Mellow Farm)

The pictures on these two pages are taken from roughly the same position, with the camera pointing in opposite directions.

Lower House Farm was renamed *Mellow Farm* by the present owner, to avoid confusion with the other *Lower House Farm* which still exists in Lindford. It is not the only confusion of names in this part of the parish (see note on Huntingford Farm opposite).

It is said that the thatched barns in the picture were renovated during the 1930s by Major Evans of Wishanger, to give people work during the depression years.

These days, the fields and facilities here are often used by youth groups and other organisations for weekend camps.

Huntingford Bridge, near Mellow Farm—1901

The River Wey is seen flowing towards the bridge along a channel which today is dry. The course later became more direct, and the field on the other side of the river bank, accessed by the gate, is now only a few yards wide. Once this happened it was known as Sunday Field, because it provided enough grazing for Sunday and was a handy distance away to collect the animals.

In the background is Huntingford Forge and Farmhouse. The Collins family were the blacksmiths here for many years. We are told that at the autumn manoeuvres of 1874, Dan Collins shoed a horse for Prince Arthur, Duke of Connaught.

There is today another Huntingford Farm in the parish, situated in Frensham Lane—nobody is quite sure when or why the name was transferred. Maps of 1938 clearly show the name still applying to the buildings here, but an earlier sale document of 1928 uses the name for the other property.

Wishanger Lodge—pre-1907

Wishanger Lodge (now renamed *Wishanger Manor*) was once the home of Mrs Branson, whose son James became a great local benefactor—Branson Road in Bordon is named after him. He was also the great-uncle of Richard Branson, the modern entrepreneur.

Interestingly, the card with the picture above was sent one Thursday in November 1907 to 10 year-old Master Ernest Chapman, son of the Grayshott builder of the same name, and nephew of Walter (see page 84).

Gorselands, built by Ernest Chapman Snr for himself, is now the 'Little Chef' café on the A3 at Bramshott Chase.

Wishanger Pond—c.1904

Neither so well-known nor so accessible as the string of ponds at Waggoners Wells, those at Wishanger have a charm of their own. They are fed largely from springs, and form a small tributary of the River Wey.

This view of the bottom pond is taken from what is now private land next to Frensham Lane. There is public access to a viewpoint of the middle pond from Bridleway No.14, which runs between Wishanger Lane and Smithfield Lane.

Frensham Pond Hotel—1902

Seen here, and from across the pond on the opposite page, the *Frensham Pond Hotel* used to be known as *The White Horse*, one of the eight inns of Headley parish that Mr Beck mentions in the Introduction. It was run by the Marden family for many years from before 1800.

Until the boundary changes of 1991, it stood in Hampshire, in the parish of Headley. Now it is in Surrey—but still in Headley as far as the Church of England is concerned. Since the advent of Parish Councils in 1894, civil and church parishes have kept separate boundaries, and this has led in many cases to anomalies arising between the two. So, until the Church Commissioners decree differently, the parish church for this hotel remains in Headley, not Frensham.

Sailing at Frensham Great Pond—1901

The pond is not natural, but was created along with several others in the 13th century to provide fish stocks for the Bishop of Winchester. These used to be drained in rotation every five years or so, and barley grown for a season on the exposed bed. It was said that this cleansed it, and prevented growths such as blue-green algae from appearing.

During the Second World War the pond was drained for a different reason—to confuse German air raiders who had it marked on their maps.

The antiquity of Headley's old parish boundary is shown by the fact that it goes in a loop along the bed of the stream which ran here before the pond was created.

Greetings from Headley, printed before 1911

We end our tour around the parish of Headley with a composition of six pictures printed in the first decade of the 20th century.

Clockwise from top left:— Lindford bridge, All Saints' Church, Headley Park, Standford ford, Headley High Street, and Headley Mill.

Note that the car at bottom centre appears to have been 'superimposed' on this and several other postcards of the time, since identical pictures can be found without it.

Acknowledgements

The following people were kind enough to help by supplying freely pictures or information for this publication:—

Sue Allden, Rita Beaven, Bob Cherry, Peter Ellis, David & Mary Fawcett, David Hadfield, Marilyn Metcalfe, Harold Nash, Doreen Parfect, Betty Parker, Rosemary Paxton, Martin Potter, Joyce Stevens, Ann Viney, Katie Warner, Jeremy Whitaker, Betty White, Anthony Williams.

If I have missed anyone from this list, please accept my apologies. So many people came forward to assist during the course of the project, and over such an extended period of time, that it was not always possible to keep a record of who contributed what.

Belated thanks, as always, must also go to the late Mr W.H. Laverty, rector of Headley parish from 1872 to 1928, whose collection of notes, maps and other information accumulated during the years of his incumbency are a constant source of joy to today's historians.

And finally, may I extend my sincere appreciation to The Headley Society for their backing and support throughout this project.

For further information on Headley and its history:—

Headley Miscellany is a series of booklets issued by The Headley Society whose aim is to make available to a wider audience the interesting and valuable historical information which exists within the parish of Headley. They are published in A5 format with illustrations, price £3.00 per booklet, available from local shops and from the Society, which may be contacted via the publisher's address at the front of this book.

List of Illustrations

✇ ✇ ✇

Other Books relating to the history of Headley

One Monday in November ... and Beyond—the story of the Selborne and Headley Workhouse Riots of 1830
During the 'Swing' riots of 1830, according to the famed historians J.L. and Barbara Hammond, "the most interesting event in the Hampshire rising was the destruction of the workhouses at Selborne and Headley." If these riots had succeeded, "the day when the Headley workhouse was thrown down would be remembered ... as the day of the taking of the Bastille." Here a local historian traces the dramatic events of two days of rioting and its aftermath in the villages and beyond.
ISBN 1-873855-33-8 Republished September 2002, Paperback, 136pp, illustrations plus maps.

All Tanked Up—the Canadians in Headley during World War II
A story of the benign 'invasion' of Headley by Canadian tank regiments over a period of four years, told from the point of view of both Villagers and Canadians. Includes many personal reminiscences and illustrations.
ISBN 1-873855-00-1 May 1994, paperback, 48pp, illustr. plus maps.

To the Ar and Back—an historical stroll around Headley and Arford
Joyce Stevens tells us the history of forty-seven locations within a mile of the centre of Headley. Illustrated with line drawings by Mick Borra. *The Headley Society, 1992, updated 2003, paperback, 26pp, illustr. plus map.*

*Headley Miscellany—a series of booklets on topics of local interest to the Village—*Using the expertise, memories and resources of residents in the parish, and also from Headley descendants spread across the world, these are of general appeal.
The Headley Society, 1999 onwards, paperback, typically 44pp

Grayshott—the story of a Hampshire village by J. H. (Jack) Smith. Written to celebrate the 75th anniversary of Grayshott Civil Parish in 1978, this book tells the history of the village from its earliest beginnings as a minor hamlet of Headley to its status as a fully independent parish flourishing on (and across) the borders of Hampshire and Surrey. *ISBN 1-873855-38-9 Originally published 1976 – republished 2002, Paperback, 210pp.*

Some Ancient Churches in North East Hampshire
—an illustrated collection of notes
Twelve fascinating churches in the north east corner of Hampshire are
described. A map on the back cover guides you through the picturesque lanes
of the area, and 33 photographs give both exterior and interior views of each
church. As well as Headley, the book includes Alton, Bentley, Binsted,
Bramshott, Froyle, Hartley Mauditt, Holybourne, Kingsley, Selborne, and East
& West Worldham. A short glossary is included for those unfamiliar with
some of the architectural terms used. Suitable size for the pocket. *ISBN 1-
873855-11-7 April 1995, Paperback, 28pp, illustrations plus map.*

On the Trail of Flora Thompson—*beyond Candleford Green*
The author of *Lark Rise to Candleford* worked in Grayshott post office
from 1898–1901, while it was still in the parish of Headley. A local
historian investigates the people and places she would have seen here at
that time. *ISBN 1-873855-24-9 May 1997, paperback, 144pp,
illustrations plus maps.*

Heatherley—*by Flora Thompson—her sequel to the 'Lark Rise' trilogy*
This is the book which Flora Thompson wrote about her time in
Grayshott. It is the 'missing' fourth part to her *Lark Rise to Candleford*
in which 'Laura Goes Further.' Full of interest to those who know this
area. Illustrated with chapter-heading line drawings by Hester Whittle.
Introduction by Ann Mallinson.
ISBN 1-873855-29-X Sept 1998, paperback, 178pp, illustr. plus maps.

The Southern Wey—*a guide by The River Wey Trust*
Covers the Southern River Wey from its source near Haslemere
through Headley parish to Tilford where it joins the northern branch.
Gives fascinating details on geology, industry, landscape and ecology
of our area. *ISBN 0-9514187-0-X Reprinted Jan 1990, paperback,
46pp, well illustrated*

Churt—*an Oasis through time*
Contains historical information of interest to our area generally, as well
as details relating to the neighbouring parish of Churt.
Olivia Cotton 1998, paperback, 100pp, illustrated

The River Running By—*a history of Standford*
John Warren—Publisher: Standford Hill Methodist Church (1986)